Prophecy Visions & Dreams

SHARON WACHOWIAK

Prophetic Clarity for God's Sons and Daughters

PROPHESY, VISIONS & DREAMS

First Printing: 2012
All rights reserved.
This book may not be copied or reprinted for commercial gain or profit. The use of short quotations or occasional page copying for personal or group study is permitted and encouraged. Permission will be granted upon request.

Unless otherwise indicated, all Scripture quotations are from The Holy Bible, New King James Version (NKJV) Scripture taken from the NEW KING JAMES VERSION®. Copyright© 1982 by Thomas Nelson, Inc. Used by permission. All rights reserved.

All pronouns referencing Jesus Christ or God are capitalized because of who He is.

Sharon Wachowiak
Lionheart Ministries International, Incorporated
1292 Crooked Creek Trail
Crown Point Indiana 46307
lionheartministries@yahoo.com

And it shall come to pass afterward, that I will pour out my spirit upon all flesh; and your sons and your daughters shall prophesy, your old men shall dream dreams, your young men shall see visions: Joel 2:28 (KJV)

CONTENTS

Chapter	Page
Introduction	*i*
The Prophet	1
Study Questions	16
Jesus the Prophet	18
Study Questions	23
Why Train Prophets	25
Study Questions	31
The Office of the Prophet/ The Prophetic Anointing	33
Study Questions	40
Who Can Be Prophetic Today	42
Study Questions	46
The Seer	48
Study Questions	56
Dreams and Visions	57
Study Questions	76
The Speaking Prophet	78
Study Questions	82

Chapter	Page
Fasting and Worship	**84**
Study Questions	**89**
A Word in Due Season	**91**
Study Questions	**98**
Manifestations	**99**
Study Questions	**102**
Proper Prophetic Release	**103**
Study Questions	**107**
False Prophets	**109**
Study Questions	**116**
Jezebel Activity	**117**
Study Questions	**125**
Conclusion	**128**
Notes	**129**

INTRODUCTION

When talking about the subject of prophecy with believers in Jesus Christ, I discovered that many of us are unaware of the prophetic Spirit He has given to us. Most of us are interested in the prophetic and believe that it should be a regular part of our spiritual life. But we mistakenly believe only a few have the privilege of hearing God's voice in this way.

Seeking the Lord for direction and encouragement is such an important part of our relationship with the Holy Spirit. Yet we often look first to others for that guidance, when it should be the other way around. Even when ministering to the broken, we may silence the promptings of the Holy Spirit, in deference to someone else we consider to be better at speaking prophetically. Although specific dominant gifts are given to God's people to express His prophetic word in the group setting, remembering that God's heart is for each of us to have a two-way relationship with Him will help us to keep balance.

Introduction

Prophetic support through others is important, and we all need the encouragement, hope, and direction found through this gift. But we need to be careful to protect ourselves from depending more on the voice of the Lord through someone else, than depending on hearing the Lord's voice personally.

Additionally, some may not realize or believe the Lord speaks to us personally except through Scripture. Perhaps, there was never an opportunity to learn about personal communion with the Holy Spirit. Or, some of us have been taught in the past that the supernatural gifts were discontinued. However, a relationship is something that comes from two persons interacting with each other. The Lord's Spirit was sent to us so we could have communion with our creator. The Apostle Paul wrote, "The grace of the Lord Jesus Christ and the love of God and the <u>communion</u> of the Holy Spirit be with you all. Amen." (2 Corinthians 13:14). The word communion in this passage is translated from the Greek word koinonia. It means to have fellowship, intimacy, community, and joint participation. This verse expresses a relationship with the Holy Spirit of Jesus Christ that is more than many of us are experiencing. Our faith as Christians is not a simple religion but a relationship with the living Christ who rose from the dead. We need to pursue Him and become aware that He is speaking to us regularly.

Our God is a prophetically, creative God who desires to reveal Himself to His people. When He tells us His plans or what He is about to do, then we become prophetic. We also have His promise. God spoke to us in Joel that in the last days, His sons and daughters would prophesy; see visions and dream dreams.[1] Peter declared in Acts 2:17 that the pouring out of the Holy Spirit on Pentecost was a fulfillment of this prophecy in Joel.[2] If these verses are true, then those of us who have been born since that first Pentecost are living in the last days to which Joel referred. In the Gospel of John, the apostle writes, "to as many as received Christ, to them He gave the

Introduction

right to become sons of God. Receiving Jesus as personal Lord and Savior gives us the privilege to become sons and daughters of God. Having a relationship with our Father through the sacrifice of Christ opens our spiritual eyes and ears to see and hear His voice.

Though some of us may minister more regularly with the Holy Spirits' gift of prophecy, all of us are a prophetic people because our Father is a prophetic God. We have inherited, through Christ, the ability to know our Father and hear His voice. Jesus said in the Gospel of John if we are His sheep, we can hear His voice and we will know Him, and we won't follow the voice of another.

The Prophet
Chapter 1

When we speak of prophets for some of us, our thoughts turn to those who are written about in the Old Testament and perhaps John the Baptist in the New Testament. Others of us might think more specifically about people such as Elijah and Elisha, David, Moses, Miriam, Huldah, Deborah, Agabus, and Philip's daughters, and others. In our present day, some speak prophetically and are accepted in the Body of Christ as prophets with a message from the Lord. Most of us have an idea of what it means to be prophetic, but we don't think about the fact that God has given us all the ability to hear Him. We don't realize that when we share what we've heard, that we are prophetic. So let's look at what the definition of a prophet might be.

The word prophet comes from an Old Testament Hebrew word with a root meaning "to bubble forth, as from a fountain," hence "to utter," comp. Ps.45:1).[3] He was a messenger of God who spoke as a forth teller

The Prophet

or oracle speaker called a Navi (נב'א), or a visionary or seer called a Roeh (ואה). The people in the culture of the days of the Old Testament expected the prophet to know the mind or will of the Lord in their present circumstances or the future. They were also sought out for direction and advice in areas such as battles, strategies, and national (governmental) crisis.[4] They were trusted to tell the future, find lost articles, perform miracles, declare warnings for sin, and act as a plumb line for righteousness.[5] Always foremost in their words was a challenge to those hearing, to draw closer to the Lord. The motivation behind the prophetic words was to cause people to turn back to God and to look for the Messiah. Although the prophets in the Old Testament had the exclusive anointing to speak and write the God-breathed Holy Scriptures, we can learn by their example how the Holy Spirit may act among us today.

The Apostle John teaches us in Revelation:

> "For the testimony of Jesus is the spirit of prophecy." (Revelation 19:10b)

When we testify about Jesus Christ, we testify by the same Spirit who spoke prophetically of the Messiah through the prophets of the Old Testament. He is the same Spirit whose job it is to convict the world of sin, righteousness, and justice, and to draw men to Christ. He still speaks encouraging words to His people and a message of hope to those who don't know Him. We are not writing scripture like the Old Testament prophets, but we are speaking the same powerful prophetic words they wrote. With this in mind, we can see how prophecy would have as its primary focus a power on it to challenge those who hear it, to draw closer to the Lord Jesus Christ. It isn't only the words but also the heart and tone of the message that draws those listening, to move toward the Lord both spiritually and naturally.

The underlying theme of the prophetic word is a message of love. That message is the Gospel. Jesus came to heal the brokenhearted and bind up their wounds; He came to open prison doors and set captives free; He came to open blind eyes, comfort the mourning, and tell everyone the good news.[6] This message of love is always within a prophetic word and is the power on the prophetic word that brings freedom. The word will establish to the listener that God is greater than the circumstances, able to move in them, and is in control of them. A sense of hope is attached to the word, even if it is convicting or includes consequences for sin. The prophetic word beckons a person to draw closer to Christ rather than rejects or condemns. That is consistent with the image that Jesus portrayed of the Father, who is always calling people to Himself.

When Christ spoke to the Samaritan women at the well, He was not in any way condemning. His words to her about her situation were true, but His tone must not have been offensive because she did not recoil in shame or run away. Even though He was a Jewish rabbi, He initiated a conversation with her. This act must have been amazing to her since the culture did not allow for Jewish men to speak to Samaritan women, especially one who was considered an outcast. Jewish minds, in that day, were full of contempt for Samaritans. She had been accustomed to being looked down upon by those around her.

The culture also demanded that a woman with her behavior would not be a part of the circle of reputable woman who may have lived in her village. She probably came to the well alone after the other women had gone so she wouldn't have to face judging eyes and condemning stares. But, here was a man who spoke to her with life-giving words as if He wasn't ashamed to speak with her and instead cared about her situation. When He invited her to drink His water, she moved toward Him emotionally. She desired more and was rewarded with the fountain of living water that flowed from His spirit. When He spoke of the worship of the Father, He acknowledged that His God and Father could be hers too. Those prophetic words were inclusive, drawing her to Him, resulting not only in her salvation but also the salvation of many in her town.[7] She felt real love from this prophet, who seemed so much like God. It must have seemed like

He knew her and everything she ever did. She even commented to her neighbors about it. It was as if He knew her inner heart and thoughts. It seemed He was there before she met Him, perhaps before she was born. This prophetic reach by Christ resulted in her amazed and excited response causing a "fountain to bubble forth" from her to her neighbors. The Messiah was there in the flesh yet somehow beyond the flesh.

God speaks to us today in the same way. The words that have been written down in scripture are spoken to us in our inner man. He speaks to us by His Spirit with the same love and gentleness. It makes sense that He would also speak through us to others the same way.

When we think of Jesus Christ, we usually mentally refer to Him within the framework of His time in the flesh when He walked the earth in Israel. We picture Him in our mind's eye with a white robe, sandals, and long hair walking down dusty country roads or riding a donkey on Palm Sunday. However, the New Testament teaches of His existence before His time among us. Jesus confirmed this when He said:

> "Verily, verily, I say unto you, before Abraham was (ever existed), I AM." (John 8:58). King James Version (KJV)

The two words "I Am" convey in the Greek and Hebrew an idea of constant, ever-present existence. It is the first person form of the Hebrew and Greek verb "to be."[8] Interestingly, Jesus didn't say, "Before Abraham ever was, <u>I was</u>." This idea conveys that He used to exist. Instead, He used the constant present tense "I Am," expressing the idea of eternal "being" even before Abraham existed. When Jesus spoke this statement to the religious leaders of His day, it meant He was in the same category with the God of their forefathers. He made Himself out to be as God. It would have caused them to remember another time God called Himself, "I AM." In Exodus 3:13-14, God spoke to Moses, a man He had assigned to free the Israelites from slavery under the Egyptians. In their conversation, Moses asked God who he should say sent him to the children of Israel. He was concerned about how this whole group of people would follow him. God told him to tell them, "I AM that I AM" sent him to them. This name conveyed to the people of Israel that the one who sent Moses to their rescue is the same God of their forefathers, including Abraham. He was the One who promised to be the God of Abraham's descendants. He is the One who was always there in their past, was present in their now, and is going to come in the future. He is the unchangeable God who is faithful and present always, therefore aware and in authority of the Israelites situation. He was then and is now the transcender of all time.

In the book of Revelation, John wrote:

> "John, to the seven churches which are in Asia: Grace to you and peace from Him <u>who is and who was and who is to come</u>, and from the seven Spirits

who are before His throne." And from Jesus Christ, the faithful witness, the firstborn from the dead, and the ruler over the kings of the earth." (Revelation 1: 4-5a).

In this passage, John refers to God the Father as the One who is, who was, and who is to come. Just a few verses further, John repeats this phrase in a prophetic utterance by Jesus Christ, God the Son:

> "I am the Alpha and the Omega, the Beginning and the End," says the Lord, "<u>who is and who was and who is to come</u>, the Almighty." (Revelation 1:8).

In this verse, John is repeating what he heard Jesus say to him about Himself, which is described in verses 11-18. He places Jesus into oneness with God the Father. Both Father and Son are the God, who was, who is, and who is to come, the "I AM." This same One was there, in the beginning, creating the world, before the covenant with Abraham and before the covenant with

Moses and the giving of the Law. Jesus declared his eternal state of being before and after time. He is the all-existent One, the "I AM." That is why the religious leaders to whom He was speaking were so angry. He made Himself equal to God.

Christ was there, before His birth, in the beginning, creating the earth and all things substance. In his letter to the Colossians, Paul declared:

> "By Him were all things created, that are in heaven, and that are in earth, visible and invisible, whether they be thrones, or dominions, or principalities, or powers: all things were created by Him and for Him. And He is before all things, and in Him, all things consist." (Colossians 1:16-17).

John also spoke of Christ's creative deity in the book of John, when He wrote:

> "In the beginning was the Word and the

Word was with God, and the Word was God. He was there in the beginning as the creator. All things were made through Him, and without Him, nothing was made that was made. And the Word became flesh and dwelt among us, and we beheld His glory, the glory as of the only begotten of the Father, full of grace and truth." (John 1:1-3, 14).

Christ is not only the fulfillment of the prophetic word spoken and written throughout the Old Testament. He is also the author of the very prophetic word He fulfilled. He became the substance of His own Holy Word spoken in the beginning at creation and throughout the ages. He is the Prophet, whose spoken anointed word had creative power on it to bring forth the manifest presence of Himself in human form. The entire creative power resident in the spoken Word of God through the mouth of His prophets waited until chronological time intersected with the divine, ordained, appointed time. At that moment, the creative life energy of the ages of God's prophetic word became flesh. Jesus Christ was and is the source of the prophetic word from Genesis to Revelation. The men who spoke and wrote the Scriptures just mouthed His creative Word and then wrote it down in a scroll. He was the One who was doing the speaking, telling them what to say from the beginning.

Jesus also called Himself the Alpha and the Omega:

> "I am the Alpha and the Omega, the
> beginning and the end," says the Lord,
> who is and who was and who is to come,
> the Almighty." (Revelation 1:8).

When we read or quote this verse, we tend to mentally skip over the alpha and omega part without really thinking about it. In the past, we've been told that this phrase means the same thing as the first and the last. So we clump the phrases together, believing Christ is just repeating the same thing only in a different way. Alpha being the first letter and omega the last letter of the Greek alphabet, it is logically easy to come to that conclusion.

Though the Hebrew and Greek languages indeed used the alphabet as a number system, I believe Jesus perhaps meant something a little different with each phrase. If we interpret this verse with a numerical viewpoint, it will read, "I am the beginning and the end, the beginning and the end," or "I am the first and the last, the first and the last." Instead, there seems to be a slight variation in thought between the two phrases. The meaning of the word "beginning" conveys an idea of origin and source.[9] Christ is the source and the origin of all things, the fountain and life flow, the Creator. The meaning of the word "end" conveys an idea of finality, the one who started everything is now the one who completes it.[10] He is the author and finisher of creation and our faith.[11]

Alpha and omega, on the other hand, relates to the alphabet and its letters, which make up all our written words. The writer of the book of Hebrews spoke of Jesus as the one who was written about from the beginning; He is the Word:

> "Then I said, 'Behold, I have come in the volume of the book it is written of Me to do your will, O God." (Hebrews 10:7).

Since Jesus is the "Word of God," it is possible that when He called Himself the Alpha and Omega, He is saying He is the first and last letter, and every other letter ever written and spoken. He is all the eternal letters and syllables that make up all the words in the Holy Scriptures. He is the whole alphabet, the word substance of the prophetic words in the Bible, but also the origin of all languages. He is the A, the Z, and all the letters in between making Him the author and source of all the Word of God. He is the Word and, therefore, the revealer of the secrets hidden in the written Word.

In 1799, the French military discovered an ancient Egyptian artifact that had an engraving of one passage translated into three different languages. One of the languages was classical Greek, which was able to be understood, enabling the other two languages of hieroglyphic and Demotic, to be deciphered. Eventually, other ancient documents were able to be translated, and the hieroglyphic and Demotic languages were unlocked. This ancient artifact is called the Rosetta Stone. The term 'Rosetta Stone' came to be used by philologists to describe any bilingual text with whose help a previously unknown language and script could be deciphered. When Jesus Christ came, He revealed the real meaning of previously misunderstood scripture. He also made visible the true character of God the Father by what He did and said. He is the Rosetta Stone, so to speak, who causes the world to be able to understand the previous undecipherable plan of God for humankind.

In the Hebrew language, the word "dabar" means "word" or "thing."[12] The word "thing" implies substance or material. In the book of John, we see a reference to Jesus as the Word:

> "And the Word (dabar) became flesh (substance/thing) and dwelt among us, and we beheld His glory, the glory as of the only begotten of the Father, full of grace and truth." (John 1:14).

The prophetic, declarative, spoken word of God became the substance of human flesh who is Jesus Christ. Jesus is our best example of what it means to be a prophet or to be prophetic. He is the first word and the last word. He also spoke the first word and will have the last word. He is the first, last, and only complete, exact Prophet of God. There is no other!

The Prophet Study Questions

1) What might the verse "the testimony of Jesus Christ is the spirit of prophecy" mean for us today? Rev.19: 10; Acts 1:8; 1 Peter 1:10-12._____

_____
_____

2) If a person receives a prophetic word that is inconsistent with the Scripture would it be ok to believe it? 2Tim. 3:16; Gal. 1:9._____ Why or why not_____

_____

_____

3) What should the underlying theme and tone of a prophetic message be and why? 1 Corinthians 13; John 4._____

_____

_____

4) Who created the world and how? Genesis 1:1-3, 26; John 1:1-3, 14; Colossians 1:13-17; Rev.4: 11._____

_____

_____

5) Explain why Jesus' activity was not limited to a particular time frame. Exodus 3:14; John1: 1-3, 14; John 8:48; Rev. 1:4, 8._____

_____

_____

Jesus the Prophet
Chapter 2

In the Old Testament, Jesus was referred to prophetically as the Messiah (anointed one) who was to come. In the New Testament, the One who was prophesied to come had arrived. His name in all languages means Salvation, the Anointed One. We know that above all else, Jesus is the Savior, the Lamb of God who takes away the sin of the world.[13] That includes everyone who ever lived, everyone who ever will live, and all of creation. However, He also referred to Himself as a prophet, and others referred to Him as a prophet or The Prophet during His time of ministry.

The Offices of Prophet, Priest, and King had been established leadership positions in the Old Testament. The expectation was that when the Messiah came; He would fulfill these three offices.[14] One of the first great initiators of the Reformation was Martin Luther.[15] He wrote that Jesus fulfilled the priestly office that consists of the satisfaction made for the sins of the world by His death on the cross. He continues in the priestly intercession of the exalted Savior for his people. John Calvin, one of the great theologians in church history, wrote that Jesus fulfilled the Kingly Office in subduing us to himself, in ruling and defending us, and in restraining and conquering all his and our enemies.[16]

Christ executes the Office of the Prophet by revealing the will of the Father to us by His Word and Spirit for our salvation, calling, guidance, and relationship with Him. Martin Luther also taught that the Prophetic Office included teaching and miracles. We only have to read Jesus' teaching from the Sermon on the Mount and read about all the miracles Jesus did to realize he fulfilled this criterion for the prophetic office as well.

The following verses confirm Christ in His prophetic office. In the book of Mathew, Jesus referred to himself as a prophet.

> "<u>A prophet</u> is not without honor except in his own country and in his own house." (Mathew 13:57).

This statement was a comment He made about Himself in response to the doubt he found among his very own family and friends.

In Luke, we also hear Jesus refer to Himself as <u>a prophet</u>:

> "Nevertheless, I must journey today, tomorrow, and the day following; for it cannot be that a prophet should perish outside of Jerusalem." (Luke 13:33).

This was a statement He made about His crucifixion in Jerusalem. We see from these verses, Jesus called Himself a prophet.

Not only did Jesus refer to Himself as a prophet, but other people in Jerusalem and the surrounding area referred to Jesus as a prophet. In the book of Luke, the two people Jesus was speaking to on the road to Emmaus, referred to Him as a prophet:

> "<u>A prophet</u> who was mighty in word and deed before God and all the people." (Luke 24:19).

In the book of John, when the people had seen all the mighty works that He was doing, they exclaimed:

> "This is truly <u>the Prophet</u> who is to come into the world." (John 6:14).

This reference was regarding the promise of God to Moses in Deuteronomy 18:18 about "another prophet" God would raise up, to whom the people would listen.

Even the Samaritans believed that Messiah would be the one who would tell all things. Meaning He was the anointed one who would speak the oracles of God. In the gospel of John, the woman at the well exclaimed to Jesus:

"I know that Messiah is coming" (who is called Christ). When He comes, He will tell us all things." (John 4:25).

In these verses, we see that others believed Jesus to be a prophet or The Prophet. They believed He was the one who had been promised to Moses and the people of Israel.

When speaking to the religious leaders, Jesus said, He didn't speak on His own authority, but He spoke by God who had sent Him.[17] He was only speaking the mind and the will of God the Father both at that present time and in the future. He was operating in the Office of Prophet.

Jesus did miracles greater than Elijah;[18] He was a plumb line of inner purity and righteousness;[19] He spoke truth into men's hearts knowing the ungodliness that was there, [20] He spoke forth the oracles of God the Father,[21] and spoke of the future.[22] He spoke prophetically about the mountain,[23] the fig tree,[24] the wind and the waves,[25] His death and resurrection of His body which would be raised after three days,[26] the days of trouble[27], and His victorious return. [28] He is not only a prophet of God, as some would say, but He is The Prophet of God for all time. He is the very material of all the prophetic word of God that has ever been and ever will be spoken. No other prophet either of time past, present, or future can usurp or super-cede His position. All prophetic utterance must be consistent with His Word spoken and written in the Holy Scripture.

Jesus the Prophet Study Questions

1) How did Jesus describe Himself in a defense of His activity to his family and friends and in response to Herod's plan, Mathew 13:57; Luke 13:31-33. _____
_____
_____
_____

2) What scripture story were the people referring to when they said "This is truly the Prophet who was to come into the world?" Deut. 18:15, 18; John 6:14; Acts 3:21-22. _____
_____
_____
_____

3) What are some of the earmarks of the Office of Prophet? Luke 24:19; John 6:14. _____
_____
_____

4) Why do you believe Jesus is the Prophet who was foretold to Moses and the people of Israel? _____
_____
_____
_____
_____
_____

Why Train Prophets
Chapter 3

Although the prophetic anointing is a supernatural gift imparted by the Holy Spirit for the work of the ministry of Christ, we cannot assume that people know how to function appropriately with it. It is important as a prophetic people to know when and how to deliver a word properly and how to receive and respond to a word given. We have seen abuses of the gift, which have given prophecy a poor reputation. Our personality quirks and personal insecurities can taint the release of this gift, resulting in negative fruit. This behavior negates the effective ministry of the Holy Spirit, and the intended result becomes thwarted. Instead, this causes damage to the hearer and propagation of negative ideas about the genuine work of the Holy Spirit.

Sometimes messages are given as prophetic words from the Lord when, in reality, they are a teaching or a personal point of view. One may be excited about something they have learned and desires to share it with the rest of the gathering. Enthusiasm about the things we learn from the Lord is a good thing, but sometimes that same enthusiasm can cause us to share what we've learned as a prophecy when it is not. Although the teaching can be appropriate for learning, it may not be an appropriate prophetic word for the corporate setting. If it is released, it often becomes a distraction rather than an enhancement to the service. At any rate, most of the hearers will know the message wasn't meant for the service because it usually falls flat rather than having the power to bring life or change.

There are also respectful protocols to follow for different places of worship. Not all meetings and churches have the same guidelines for the delivery of a prophetic word. Some churches allow speaking out from the congregation. Others ask that prophetic words to be prescreened by a point person previously chosen by the leadership. Still, other churches do not allow a prophetic word to be spoken during the worship service. Many pastors and leaders have changed the way a prophetic word is released to their respective congregations. An unpleasant experience with a prophetic person's delivery has called for new guidelines. Those who insist on releasing a word "their way" and then excusing themselves by stating "God told me" have caused the prophetic voice to be damaged rather than supported.

As we learn to be respectful of leadership and guidelines for places of worship, the prophetic voice will be given room for expression without suspicion. Training can be done through classes or seminars, or by mentoring and orientation.

The appropriate timetable for releasing a prophetic word is something we can learn, as well. Many times God will give a prophetic word that is important for that moment because the hearts of the people are open to receive it right then. On other occasions, God will give a prophetic word ahead of time. When this happens, often, the person may immediately want to release it. But, releasing a word at the wrong time can hinder the acceptance of the word. The prophetic vision that was given to Daniel about the end of days was given long before it could be understood. God told Daniel to close up the vision to prevent it from being given until its appointed time. The timing was extremely important to God. The prophetic word today can come under the same guidelines as the scriptural examples given in the Bible concerning prophecy. As we study prophetic release, especially in the New Testament, we can gain balance and wisdom as to how the prophetic functions, now.

Properly receiving a prophetic word is as important as releasing one. There is a responsibility on the hearers of a prophetic word to respond appropriately to it. A word should be discerned spiritually as well as tested with the heart and word of scripture. We have heard stories about a prophecy commanding someone to sell all they have or quit their job and move to Africa to become a missionary. While this sounds like a good thing to do, and many people have done it at the Lord's leading, a word like this from someone else must be confirmed by other means, as well. We can ask the Lord to confirm it in scripture, obtain other's counsel, or ask for additional confirming words. Most often, a prophetic word will confirm what we already know the Holy Spirit is revealing to us.

All too often, the responsibility for the result of a prophetic word is placed entirely on the prophetic speaker. But the hearer has a responsibility for their response as well. When I was young and had gotten into trouble for misbehaving with my siblings or friends, I would say to my parents, "so and so told me to do it." My mother would often respond with a very simple phrase that I'm sure affected my individuality when I grew older. She would say, "If someone told you to jump into the lake and drown, would you?" That simple phrase spoken to me over and over taught me to think for myself. Because someone tells me to do something or to go somewhere, doesn't mean I ought to do it. Training in this area will help allay fears and improper responses when the prophetic voice is operating.

In the Old Testament in I Samuel 19:20, Samuel was appointed over the school of the prophets of his day. Samuel was a leader/prophet of great anointing and character and was chosen by the Lord for his position. There were schools or colleges of the prophets found in Naioth[29] Gilgal,[30] Bethel[31], and Jericho.[32] We see that it was necessary to lead other prophets for proper training. In I Kings 19:16, we see the Lord told Elijah to anoint Elisha to be a prophet in his place. Later, Elijah threw his mantle on Elisha, who left everything to serve Elijah. Elijah gave personal orientation and mentoring to Elisha, who learned and followed his example until he was ready to become a prophet in his own standing. In the New Testament, Paul took time in 1 Corinthians 12-14 to teach on all the gifts of the Spirit, one of them being prophecy. He also taught the proper release for these gifts in this New Testament Church, which operated in all the supernatural gifts of the Spirit. We see from these passages that although prophecy is imparted supernaturally by the Holy Spirit, how we handle this anointing is related to training and proper understanding and delivery of the gift.

Why Train Prophets Study Questions

1) Name some examples of prophetic training in the Old Testament? I Kings 19:16, 19-21; I Samuel 19:19-24. _____
_____
_____
_____
_____

2) What is an example of prophetic training in the New Testament? _____
_____
_____
_____
_____

3) How can the prophetic anointing be enhanced through training?
_____
_____
_____
_____

**4) What would be the proper action if you received a prophetic word in an unfamiliar gathering?
I Corinthians 14:32; Hebrews 13:17** _____
_____
_____
_____
_____

The Office of the Prophet versus the Prophetic Anointing
Chapter 4

Understanding the difference between the Office of the Prophet and a prophetic anointing is important because they are defined differently in scripture. As the official vocational ministry gifts that Jesus gave the church become increasingly understood, clarity of their respective characteristics and interrelationship will be needed.

The Office of the Prophet is one of the members of the set of ministry gifts, as stated by Paul in Ephesians 4:11. This official gift has become more present in the Church within the last fifty years. It is more recognized and accepted as a present part of the ministerial team of Apostle, Evangelist, Pastor, and Teacher. The Gift of Prophecy is inherent in both the Office of the Prophet and the prophetic anointing. The

Prophetic office is a more official role of ministry in the Church than the general prophetic anointing, which is on every believer. Even those who may function more dominantly with the Gift of Prophecy, as discussed in I Corinthians 12: 10, may not necessarily be in the official prophetic role. The Office of Prophet relates positional to the Church in a more professional way, although, at present, it is not yet fully established as the Pastor or Evangelist offices have. The Office of Prophet relates specifically to the church as a whole, or church leaders corporately or globally in a governmental way.

Let's look at the Office of Pastor to understand the Office of Prophet better. The Pastor of a church or institution who holds the position or office of Pastor relates to the congregation as a whole. His leadership is for the corporate body. He may minister to individual people in his congregation, but his general focus is on the condition of the whole flock and how to meet their needs. He functions in a governmental way to his local congregation or satellite congregations.

This office is often vocational and is a respected position and holds a level of influence that is not held by other individuals in the congregational group. The pastor carries weightiness in his leadership position, and his decisions and vision greatly influence the direction of the church or organization. The Office of Pastor interrelates with the other official ministerial gifts, by bringing unity to the congregation and a vision to do the work of the ministry. The Office of the Prophet works similarly.

This office also works within the structure of the other four Ministry Gifts, comparable to the Office of Pastor. The Office of the Prophet often supports the apostolic vision of the church group or leaders prophetically either locally or globally. The Office of the Prophet also speaks governmentally to the direction that the pastor, apostle, or church group/denomination needs to take. If there is a tendency toward misalignment in established vision or scope, the person in the Office of the Prophet often addresses return or realignment to the vision of the Lord.

There is a weightiness the Office/Position carries regarding recognition by the leadership that is not always present with a prophetic anointing. The Prophet in the Office may also lead unbelievers to Christ; however, their prophetic voice is usually spoken to leaders in various positions in the church or nations.

The anointing of prophecy operates supernaturally with the gift of prophecy, as does the Office of Prophet. However, this gift operates more among the general population of the church or with unbelievers. The prophetic words often have the same characteristics as the Office, but the focus is generally on the individual or small group. The gift of prophecy is an adjunct gift to aid the believers to do the ministry of Christ in the same way He walked the streets and ministered to people. The anointing of prophecy can be used to bring healing and deliverance, and to speak prophetically to unbelievers to bring them to Christ.

In the Old Testament, both Daniel and Samuel operated in the Office of Prophet. Daniel had directional influence and prophetic recognition with kings that related to the circumstances surrounding their respective pagan nations. Samuel was an apostolic prophet who administered legal judgment and justice to the nation of Israel, similar to our Supreme Court Justices today. Until he anointed Saul to be king, he was the governmental authority. However, when a king was in place, Samuel still operated in the Office of Prophet, speaking correction, and justice to the activities of the king and the nation of Israel. He eventually prophesied and was involved with Saul's removal and David's installation as king. Samuel gave clear direction and correction to the leaders and the people corporately leading them by the Word of the Lord. In our day, all the major and minor prophets of the Old Testament still hold the Office of Prophet to the Church. Their prophetic words became much of the scripture, which is given to us for our instruction and example for Christian living. We also use their written words in Scripture as a standard for prophecies today. Even though the prophetic vocational office functions in the church today as a leadership influence, it is still governed by the prophets who wrote the Scripture.

The prophetic anointing found in the Old Testament can be seen in a story about King Saul. In 1 Samuel 10:1-13, Saul was chosen and anointed to become King of Israel. Samuel told Saul he would become a new man when the Spirit of the Lord came upon him. As Saul was returning to his home, he happened on a company of prophets just as Samuel had prophesied. When Saul came among them and under the prophetic anointing, he began prophesying. Although Saul was not a prophet, when he was under the Spirit of prophecy, he was able to prophesy within that anointing.

In the New Testament, we also see two kinds of prophets. In Acts 11:28, Agabus, acting in the Office, prophesied to the church that there would be a famine in the known world. Responding to this word from the Lord, the leaders decided to send relief according to their ability to those who were in Judea. This word was governmental in that the leaders responded, and the church moved corporately in benevolent work.

In Luke 2:36-38, we see the prophetic anointing at work. Anna was a prophetess who fasted and prayed at the temple for many years. I imagine though it does not say that she was also looking for the Messiah's soon birth. She was known as a prophetess, so she must have given prophetic words before the situation we read about in Luke. When she saw Jesus, she praised and thanked the Lord, then proceeded to direct all who came into the temple to Christ, calling Him the Redemption. Her prophetic word ministered to individuals in the general temple population. It also directed people toward the Lord, the Messiah.

We see from these examples that though the focus of the two prophets is different, the character and tone of the prophetic gifting is the same. What is being spoken today by those who move dominantly with the gift of prophecy are most often moving with the prophetic anointing rather than under the auspices of the Office of the Prophet. Generally, a prophet who is holding the Office today is identified by the focus and caliber of the Word of the Lord he or she releases and the influence their prophetic words have on the people. The prophetic words and acts themselves will establish the prophet as one who holds the Prophetic Office.

The Prophetic Office versus The Prophetic Anointing Study Questions

1a) How is the prophetic anointing different than the prophetic office? Eph.4: 10-13; Acts 11:27-30; Acts 21:8-13; 1 Corinthians 12-14. _____
_____
_____
_____

2) What are some of the earmarks of the prophetic office that are the same as the prophetic anointing?
_____
_____

_____
_____
_____
_____

3) How is the Office of the Prophet identified considering the acceptance of the five offices? Proverbs 18:16. _____
_____
_____
_____
_____

4) What kind of prophets were Samuel, Daniel, and Agabus? 1 Samuel 7:3; Daniel 2:16; Acts 11:29.
_____
_____
_____
_____
_____

Who Can Be Prophetic
Chapter 5

When our children are born, we expect them to have both eyes and ears. God gave us these organs to enable us to see and to hear. Most of our growth and learning in the early years come from our parents, so our eyes and ears become sensitive to their faces and voices. As humans, we begin recognizing our parents' voices at a very early age. Except in certain circumstances, most humans can see and hear. These senses help us navigate more skillfully in our daily lives.

In Psalm 94:9, the Lord makes it known to us that He made our eyes and ears to see and hear, and that since He made them, He is the best at seeing and hearing. He was speaking to his people on a spiritual level. Since God is spirit, He listens naturally with his spiritual ears and sees naturally with His spiritual eyes.

If we look at the natural physical man, we have a hint as to how God may relate to us spiritually. Paul writes in Romans 1:9 that we should see the invisible attributes of God in all of nature (everything made). In this passage, Paul refers to many people having natural eyes to <u>see</u> God. When we have a spiritual rebirth, I believe the expectation God has as a father is that we would have spiritual eyes and ears to see and hear His voice. These spiritual organs help us navigate much more skillfully through our spiritual walk and call with Jesus.

It's interesting to note that prophets in the Old Testament were called both seers and prophets. Seers saw God's purposes, and prophets spoke God's purposes as they heard Him. Both had to have spiritual eyes and ears that were sensitive to the Spirit of the Lord. All of us who have a personal relationship with Jesus should be able to hear and see the Lord's voice and purposes. Jesus said in John 10:27, His sheep hear His voice, and they recognize it and they don't follow the voice of another. We are a prophetic people who by Jesus' word should be able to see and hear what He is saying. We can then bring His voice to those around us, both those who know Him and those who don't.

Testifying to an unbeliever about Jesus or declaring His Word during prayer moves us into that prophetic flow, but we need to be listening for the voice of His Spirit. Remember, the testimony of Jesus Christ is the Spirit of Prophecy. In Joel 2:28, the writer declared that in the Day of Christ, God would pour out His Spirit on <u>all flesh,</u> and His <u>sons and daughters would prophesy.</u> Peter declared on the Day of Pentecost when the Holy Spirit was poured out on the believers, that what was happening at that moment referred back to the prophecy of Joel.[33] Those of us who have been born since then should prophesy according to that word. We may not all function prophetically in the same way. Some of us may minister more dominantly with the gift, but all of us are a prophetic people in one way or another. If we have received Jesus as our Savior, we are sons and daughters of God. As children of God, we have the inherited privilege of receiving the empowering work of His Holy Spirit, which places us under His prophetic anointing.

We know that prophecy is the forth speaking or foretelling the messages and the word of God. Therefore when we use the scriptures in our intercession or when we speak what we have heard the Lord say, we are acting prophetically.

There is creative power on the prophetic word to set in motion the natural realm to begin moving forward, to cause the natural circumstances to come into alignment with the Kingdom of Heaven Will of God. This power is the combination of the Word- Jesus Christ, who is engaged with the Holy Spirit to cause circumstances to change and come into alignment with the Kingdom of Heaven Will of God the Father for us and others. The purposes of God are then made to appear and be accomplished on the earth and in our lives. In the beginning, this is what occurred at creation, and this is still what occurs when we speak the Word in a prophetic, declarative way. We see this in the Lord's Prayer when He teaches us to call the Kingdom of God to come, and the Will of God to be done on the earth in our circumstances as it is already and freely done in heaven.

As sure as light came into existence when God spoke by the Word (Jesus Christ), and said; "let there be light" both at the beginning of creation, and when Jesus was conceived as the Light of the World, so the written and spoken word of the Lord is as powerfully creative today in Jesus' name. Each one of us in the Body of Christ has been given a prophetic anointing to declare the creative Word of the Lord into our circumstances, families, towns, cities, nations, and world.

Who Can Be Prophetic Study Questions

1) Who can be prophetic today in the Body of Christ and why? John 10:27; Joel 2:28-29; 1 Corinthians 12, 14._____
_____

2) What does seeing and hearing have to do with prophecy? John 10:3-5 _____

2) How can prophecy advance the kingdom? Mt.1: 19-24; Luke 2: 36-38; John 5:16, 19-20. _____

_____ Hint: Is God's Word still creative?

3) How can prophecy help with leading people to the Lord Jesus as personal Savior? John 4:4-39. _____

The Seer
Chapter 6

Visions and dreams have always been a part of God's language to humanity. God was and is the first visionary. When He created humankind, I'm sure He envisioned what we would be like before He created us, not unlike the way an artist envisions his masterpiece before he puts it down on canvas. Attached to every human life are a purpose and a vision that God desires to see embraced and fulfilled. Jeremiah described this vision that the Lord has for us:

> "For I know the plans that I think toward you, says the LORD, plans of peace, and not of evil, to give you a hope and a future." (Jeremiah 29:11)[34]

God is our seer who knows who we are, where we are, and what our need is at every moment. However, He also sees us for what He intends us to become. His seer ability goes to every facet of who He created us to be. Hagar found this out when she was sent away with Ishmael into the wilderness. God showed her where there was a well of water so she and Ishmael would not die of thirst. He met her and her son's immediate need. He also reminded her of a promise He gave her years earlier when she was pregnant, about the future of her son. Her understanding of His great ability to know her and her son's need and where she was in the wilderness, caused her to respond to Him with a hallowed title. She called the place Beer Lahai Roi, which means; the Well of the Living One, who is my Seer or who sees me. She also understood that at her and her son's lowest time, when all her hope was gone, God again gave her a visual promise of hope for the future. He was her "Seer" in both senses of the word.[35] He saw and responded to her circumstances, meeting her immediate need. He then spoke as a seer to her about her son's future, restoring her hope in His promise.

God, in His visionary character, speaks in

symbolism. He created the Hebrew people who culturally relate in symbolic ways. As Christians, we become familiar with this way of relating to each other by receiving the scriptures as our own. The symbolism in Scripture became a part of the Christian culture from the beginning of our in grafting into the Kingdom of God. Even today, when understanding the scripture and sacraments, new believers begin thinking symbolically. In the Lord's Supper, we see the bread and wine as symbols of the broken body and blood of our Savior. References to water and oil are understood symbolically to mean the flow and anointing of the Holy Spirit. One of the signs of the presence of the Messiah is that signs and wonders would confirm His authenticity. God is a sign man, and sign is one of the languages He uses to speak to us.

In our modern culture, a hearing-impaired person uses an alternate method of communication. We call this sign language. The fingers, hands, and body do all the speaking. This language is seen rather than heard but is no less a language than the spoken word. The symbols and gestures have meanings for words known to everyone who understands sign language. This type of communication is not unlike the symbolic way God spoke with His people in Scripture and still speaks with His people today. In His grace, He releases His sign language form of communication to us and then gives us the visionary ability to see and begin to understand it. God gives the seer the ability to gain revelation through seeing pictures via visions or dreams.

The secrets and helpful hints the Lord gives us can be seen with our spiritual eyes in our mind. Or, they can also be seen as an actual reality with our eyes open. When we see with our mind's eye, it is called a closed vision. When we see with our eyes open as if it were happening, it is called an open vision. When talking of his experience of being taken up into the third heaven, Paul couldn't tell if he was dreaming or experiencing reality. His attempt to explain what he saw was preceded with a question in his mind. He could not tell if he was in the body or out of the body.[36] In this case, Paul did not know if he had an open or closed vision. Both kinds of "seeing" are God-given abilities to see into the spiritual realm; one kind of vision does not have more value than the other. Both are God's way of speaking to man. In Job 33: 14-16, God tells us that He speaks to us in visions in the night first one-way and then another to instruct man upon his bed.

In the seer aspect of the prophetic anointing, visions are received and seen, metaphorically. The visions and dreams received may be pictures of everyday circumstances that have a different interpretation than what is culturally understood. God's way of speaking in metaphors is not unlike the parabolic language that Jesus used to teach during His time in the flesh. In Genesis 40: 1-10, while Joseph was in prison, he interpreted the dreams of Pharaoh's butler and baker. Although both dreams were about occurrences of everyday life in their culture, both dreams had a symbolic interpretation of a literal event that was about to occur in each of their respective lives. In the butler's dream, three branches meant three days; in the baker's case, three baskets meant three days. Although branches and baskets were known articles of use in the dreams, they represented a different symbolic meaning.

Webster's Dictionary defines a metaphor as:

> 1: A figure of speech in which a word or phrase literally denoting one kind of object or idea is used in place of another to suggest a likeness or analogy between them (as in drowning in money); broadly: figurative language.

In Acts 10:10-16, Peter's vision about unclean food was metaphoric with a spiritual meaning. Although the Lord was giving him a picture of unclean food, this did not mean that God wanted Peter to get up and start eating these different non-kosher meats. Instead, this vision referred, as we know, to the inclusion of the gentile people groups in the Kingdom of God. Peter saw one thing, but what he saw meant something else with an instructional truth within it. Eventually, Peter was led by the Holy Spirit through circumstances and obedience to understand the meaning of the vision.

As we receive metaphoric pictures, it is our responsibility to seek the Lord for the interpretation of what He has given us. This seeking can be done by the prophet or by the recipient of the message of God. When in a group of people, it is always helpful for the metaphoric prophet or "seer" to ask the Lord for a quick interpretation so all can understand what the Lord is saying. Sometimes a seer prophet can see something in the spirit that may sound very strange to someone who may be unfamiliar with metaphoric or spiritual messages. For example, recently, while in a prayer group, I saw a large hawk next to one of the people in the group. Every time this person wanted to move out into new things, this hawk would put out its wing to prevent the person from moving forward. I knew by the Spirit that something had happened in his past that had caused him to be unable to move forward in what God had for him. While this picture I saw was true, I couldn't just say, "I see a hawk next to you putting its wing in your way." I had to interpret that message so the person could understand it without it sounding strange. In I Corinthians 12: Paul speaks of the importance of understanding what is being said when there is a message spoken in tongues. He writes that there must be an interpretation of that message for the benefit of all. The same standard can be applied to this form of communication from the Lord. If a vision is received in metaphoric language during corporate worship, how can anyone understand unless there is an interpretation? When the apostle John received the revelation of Jesus Christ on the Isle of Patmos, many of the symbols were recognized by the Jewish people of that day. However, several of the symbols needed supernatural interpretation, much the same way Jesus interpreted many of His parables to His disciples. The same is true for this seer gifting.

The Seer Study Questions

1) What is a Seer? 2 Chron. 9:29; Deut. 13:1-3; Is. 30:10; 1 Kings 22:19; Isaiah 6:1; Amos 9:1. _____
_____
_____
_____
_____

2) What is the difference between a Seer and a Prophet? I Chron. 29:29; 2 Chron. 12:15; Isaiah 30:10. _____
_____
_____
_____

3) How did God reveal Himself to Hagar? Gen. 16:6-14; Gen. 21:14-20. _____
_____
_____
_____
_____

4) Why does God speak to us in symbols? Job 33:14-18; Ps. 16:7; Acts 10:10-16. _____
_____
_____
_____

5) How is the language of a Seer like one of the supernatural gifts of the Holy Spirit? 1 Cor. 14:5-6. ____
_____
_____
_____

Dreams and Vision
Chapter 7

A few years ago, I dreamed I was in a big auditorium listening to a choir on stage singing about a baby boy born to us who was our salvation. My niece was one of the singers but also on stage was another young girl who was the exact twin of my niece. I leaned over to my sister, who is my niece's mother, and commented about how much alike they looked. My sister agreed but then stated that my niece never really liked her. In the dream, my niece belonged to a very conservative denomination, and her look-alike belonged to a full gospel church. I responded to my sister's comment with, "that's too bad because look, they are all singing the same song." The interpretation came the next morning. Though there is some conflict between evangelicals and charismatics, Christ's heart is that we become one and look more to our sameness rather than our differences. We all have a heart to share the gospel and reach the lost. God sees us with the same heart and wants us to be in unity because we all have and speak about Jesus as the Savior. We all sing the same song or speak the same language.

I have a friend who had a dream he was about to die, and many people were throwing dirt on him as if to bury him, although he was not yet dead. In our modern language, the phrase "to throw dirt on someone" implies talking about and slandering someone behind their back. Here is the interpretation of that dream. He was going through a hard place at that time and felt like he was on the verge of dying emotionally. However, instead of his friends and family encouraging him, they were talking negatively behind his back. They were as we say, "throwing dirt on him."

God often uses the language we are familiar with to speak to us, even if it is in a metaphor. In Jeremiah 1:11, 12, Jeremiah received a vision of the almond branch. The Lord used a symbol with which Jeremiah was familiar. In Hebrew thought of that day, the almond branch symbolized a new, early thing, because it was one of the first trees to bloom when spring arrived, often blooming in February. The word itself means wakeful hastening. The Lord said He is "watching over His word to perform it," implying ever wakeful and hastening early to accomplish it. Jeremiah understood what the Lord was saying to him because the symbolic meaning of the almond branch was part of his culture.

God also speaks to us in dreams in the night. These are called night visions. We are often so busy, and our minds are so full of what we have to do that it is difficult to hear the Lord speaking to us during our waking hours unless we are particularly tuned in. He waits until our spirits and minds our quiet to speak to us in the night that which we could not hear during the day. Another reason He will speak to us in the dark is that the day and the night are the same to him. According to Psalm 139:12, light is revelation that pierces the darkness and brings us understanding. Revelation is given to us for instruction, encouragement, direction, and warning. God gives us dreams and visions in the night to remind us that the night is not dark to Him, and He is Lord over both day and night. He not only sees us where we are but also reveals another facet of Himself to us right in the middle of the night. We do not have to be afraid in the dark. He sees us as plain as day and enlightens us when the darkness surrounds us.

When God speaks to us in metaphors, He often uses symbols He has used in Scripture. As we study the Scripture, we can become familiar with some of these symbols. For instance, when He spoke of the Temple or of Israel corporately, He would often call it "my house." We see this in Isaiah:

> "Even them will I bring to my holy mountain and make them joyful in <u>MY HOUSE</u> of prayer: their burnt offerings and their sacrifices shall be accepted upon my altar; for <u>MY HOUSE</u> shall be called a house of prayer for all people."(Isaiah 56:7).

He also used the word house to indicate a particular family or generation of people:

> "Neither showed they kindness to the HOUSE of Jerubbaal, namely, Gideon, according to all the goodness which he has shown unto Israel." (Judges 8:35).

On occasion, the Lord used the word "house" to indicate a particular structure or spiritual stronghold. We also see in Judges that He used the word "house" to describe the structure of bondage in Egypt that the children of Israel dwelt in:

> "That the LORD sent a prophet unto the children of Israel, which said unto them, Thus says the Lord God of Israel, I brought you up from Egypt and brought you forth out of the HOUSE of bondage." (Judges 6:8).

Learning some of the symbols in the Scripture can aid us when we are presented with a dream that needs interpretation.

Knowing all the metaphoric symbols, the Lord might use extends far beyond the scope of this book. However, for training's sake, I will list a few metaphoric examples that I have come to know through the Holy Spirit's guidance with interpretation.

- **Large houses** and buildings often mean ministries, churches or denominations
- **Smaller houses** generally mean the local family or extended family
- **Houses** can also mean spiritual structures that are established in a family, area, city, church, denomination, etc. Their size or range of influence would be expressed by the size of the house in the dream or vision. A spiritual structure can be a house of witchcraft, a house of control, a house of addiction or drugs, a

house of salvation, a house of peace, a house of life, etc.

- **Ships,** buses, semi type trucks, and the like often represent national ministries or global ministries that are more mobile in scope rather than local or stationary churches.
- **Cars** often represent an individual's personal walk with the Lord.
- **Spiders**, snakes, and other reptiles often indicate a demonic presence or witchcraft.
- **Darkness** often indicates depression, oppression, or evil.
- **Black and white** clothing or cars can also represent the prophetic, or news media.
- **Blue** represents the Holy Spirit, revelation, or heavenly things. (the sky is blue) Negatively it means depression. ("I feel blue" means feeling down or depressed).
- **Green** means new beginnings, a new thing, or go forward. (Every spring new plants grow up from the ground. The color green in a stoplight

means go). Negatively, green can mean envy or jealousy. (Green with envy).
- **Purple** usually means royalty or priestly stance.
- **Red or Crimson** usually means the blood of Jesus or wisdom.
- **Yellow** represents God's glory, light, or love. Negatively yellow can mean cowardice. (He's yellow is an idiom for being a coward.

There are many more symbols the Lord uses to speak to us; these few are written here so that the idea of interpretation can be better understood. Although symbols in a dream may have a natural meaning, they can also have a spiritual meaning that has nothing to do with the natural. Seeking the Lord for the sure interpretation helps us to receive clarity as to its meaning. Many times the interpretation of a dream or vision is released supernaturally much the same way the supernatural gift of Interpretation of Tongues is released. Common symbols then may take on a completely new meaning, which is different from the usual meaning of a symbol. Have you ever read a verse in the Bible that gave you fresh revelation about its meaning even though you read that verse many times before? Dream interpretation operates much the same way. Even though a common symbol has meant a particular thing a few times before, God may use it to mean something new this time. Therefore, it is important to seek the Lord for His thought on the vision or dream. He is the one who gave it to you, and He is the one who knows what it means and what He wants you to know.

As was stated earlier, there are two different ways that one might receive a vision or dream. Most visions and dreams that are from the Lord are perceived by spiritual eyesight through closed vision. The pictures that the Lord gives are seen in the mind's eye with clarity or as an impression. The vision is seen without the use of the natural eye but with the eyes of the spirit. Sometimes the Lord opens the spirit realm to the natural eye so that visions or dreams are perceived as a natural reality. It is as if the events given in the vision or dream are happening in the natural realm and are seen as a natural reality with the eyes open, thus the name open vision. When receiving this type of vision, it is sometimes difficult to discern whether the events are happening in the spirit or if one is participating in the vision literally. Although the events of this type of vision are seen and experienced as a reality, they are no more or less valid than those that are perceived by the spirit. Both types of visions and dreams are of equal value and importance. They are both given for the various purposes stated previously.

Night visions are visions that are received from the Lord while we sleep. We may call these phenomena, dreams, rather than night visions, because that is our cultural description. However, dreams from the Lord are usually very vivid in color and very detailed. They are often imprinted on our memory so that we can recall many of the details after waking. While this is most often the case, there are always exceptions to the rule.

Sometimes we may receive a dream from the Lord that we cannot remember. King Nebuchadnezzar is one example. Although his dream was from the Lord, he was unable to remember it or interpret it. He needed Daniel, who sought the Lord for the dream and the interpretation, to remind him of his dream. Nebuchadnezzar was not a Jew but a pagan whom the Lord saw fit to speak to in the night. We see this gracious expression of the Lord throughout Scripture. Many unbelieving gentiles were told secrets from the God they did not even worship. This activity is probably true today in light of the verse in Joel that states that in the last days, God would pour out His Spirit on ALL flesh.

It is our job as children and friends of our God to seek Him for the interpretation of our dreams and the dreams of those around us who might not know Him.

Dreams are one of the vehicles God uses to reach someone with His grace and love. One might ask why He doesn't just speak in our plain everyday language. God desires us to seek Him, and this is one of the ways He engages us. I also believe He is a God of mystery and adventure. When I was young, I loved reading mystery books such as Nancy Drew and The Hardy Boys. I often tried to figure out the end from the hints in the books. This is what I believe when we have dreams and visions. The Lord presents little hints that cause us to seek more understanding; in the process, we find ourselves in a relational adventure with Him.

On occasion, we may not receive the interpretation of a dream for weeks or months. Later, when the events of the dream have begun to unfold, the Lord will bring the dream back to us and then release the interpretation. Similarly, this is how Peter responded to the release of the Holy Spirit on the day of Pentecost when he exclaimed, "This is that which was spoken by the prophet Joel." When Joel prophesied to Israel, he did not know what it was going to look like when it happened. He may have even reasoned in his mind how it would come to pass. However, the true meaning of the interpretation of that prophetic word did not happen until years later on the day of Pentecost when the Holy Spirit was released in power after Jesus' ascension. This is one of the ways He works today. Sometimes God will say to us, "this is that dream that you had," perhaps months or years after it was first received. He will often tell us something long before the fulfillment of it. Waiting develops patience and faith, but it also encourages us to intercede and pray into the fulfillment of the prophetic word.

It is also helpful if one awakens after a dream to have a pen and notebook readily available so the dream or vision can be written down. Recording the dream prevents it from being forgotten the next morning. God often supports this by waking us after a night vision. Writing it down brings clarity and seals the details so that they can be shared with others later. Gaining understanding through sharing our visions maintains a level of safety and often brings a sound interpretation. God speaks of this in Habakkuk:

> "And the LORD answered me, and said, WRITE THE VISION, and make it plain upon tablets that he may run who reads it." (Habakkuk 2:2).

The word "run" here implies a quick response as a messenger of the vision. In other words, he will go and tell others. When shared, night visions can bring instruction and direction to the rest of us. They can also reveal God's personal nature to those who don't know Him and who would not otherwise be able to hear His voice.

Some dreams or visions that come from the Lord do not need an interpretation. These dreams come as literal events. There are many instances in the Scripture where God gave a dream in plain language. God spoke to Joseph, the earthly father of Jesus, more than once in plain language in a vision or a dream.

When he was going to put Mary away for being unfaithful, the Lord spoke very clearly to Joseph to take Mary as his wife. God confirmed Mary's story. Later, when Christ was in danger, God told Joseph in a dream to go to Egypt. In both cases, Joseph understood clearly and immediately obeyed the message. Zechariah, while in the temple offering incense, saw a clear vision of an angel who told him about the conception and birth of his son, John the Baptist. The vision came in the language Zechariah knew. When we receive a vision or dream in plain language, we still need to make sure the dream is from the Lord. Asking for confirmation through His Word, another prophetic word, or through wise counsel helps determine that.

Not all dreams are messages from the Lord. There are times our soul man will dream a dream to work out something that may be bothering us during the day. These dreams are often in faded color and may be vague in meaning or come in bits and pieces. Interpretation of these dreams is more difficult because they are not always easily remembered and come in fragments. If a dream does not receive an interpretation and is not a reoccurring dream, it is best not to lose sleep over it. Release it to the Lord or put it on the shelf and move on. God may bring the meaning later on.

On occasion, soul dreams can be vivid and may be reoccurring. These dreams are usually related to some trauma or unresolved stress situation that has happened previously in the person's life. Dreams like this may produce anxiety or fear in the individual, and may not go away until the conflict is resolved, through healing, deliverance, counseling, or time.

The last type of dream one may have is related to the enemy of our souls. Satan despises man and enjoys tormenting him. He will try to bring confusion or fear and worry to our mind to rob us of our peace. In 1 Peter, Peter warns us about this when he said:

"Be sober, be vigilant; because your

adversary the devil, as a ROARING LION, walks about, seeking whom he may devour." (1 Peter 5:8).

We need to be alert to the enemy's strategies by recognizing the earmarks of his attempts to discourage us. When Satan is the source of a dream, it will often be in black and white or gray and will cause confusion, anxiety, and fear. These dreams may be remembered the next day but are not be able to be interpreted with logical understanding. Just as Satan masquerades as an angel of light during the day, he also deceives by dreams at night[37]. That is why it is of utmost importance to seek the Lord about the dream and the interpretation. In the process, He will also let you know if the dream was from Him or the devil.

Several years ago, I was at a meeting where a woman started to shout the name of Jesus at a time when the Holy Spirit was moving in a very quiet way. This activity quenched the Holy Spirit's activity in the room and caused much distraction. During this moment, I was reminded of the verse in Luke 4:11 that describes how evil spirits cried out after Jesus, saying He was the Son of God.[38] This word may sound genuine but is a spirit of darkness that is subtly trying to connect itself with truth to deceive. The feeling many of us had that day was that this was one of those times. I moved over toward the woman quietly, whispering in her ear for this dark spirit to leave her. She immediately ran from the room and did not return for the rest of the night. The next day she was there again and proceeded to do the same thing she had done the night before. This time, the speaker rebuked this spirit from the pulpit. The woman ran from the room, embarrassed and very upset. Two weeks later, I had a dream that came in some detail but was dim in color. In the dream, I was in a room with the same speaker of that day and the leader of the meeting. They proceeded to tell me it wasn't the woman who needed deliverance, but instead, it was I who had a demon. I said ok and sat down in a chair for the two of them to pray for me. Suddenly, my forehead opened up, and fruit started shooting out like a machine gun. The fruit hit the wall and smashed dripping down the wall. The dream ended, leaving me with a very strong sense of hopelessness and discouragement. I felt that all the fruit I had ever released in the Lord's Name was without success. Instead of my fruit prospering, it had hit a wall and was smashed. This feeling hung around for several days. Finally, after seeking the Lord with others, it was revealed that this woman was angry at the circumstances of that day and had sent a curse, which became a dream that caused discouragement to me. When the source of that dream was revealed, we prayed for the woman and broke the curse sent to me, which caused the dark feeling to leave.

Even though this was a dream sent from the enemy, it had a small amount of power to affect me in the area of my emotions. Nevertheless, because of the faithfulness of our protecting Father, it could not remain or prosper. If we seek the Lord, in His faithfulness, He will always reveal the truth to us. As our father, He is our protector and instructor. This dream eventually was turned into good, as I was able to gain experience in recognizing one of the wiles of the devil.

Discerning the fruit produced by dreams and visions becomes a safety net because it enables us to recognize the source. If a dream produces fear, discouragement, depression, or distraction away from the call of the Lord, it is generally demonic. This test is one of the safety guidelines for all types of prophetic utterance.

Dreams and Visions
Study Questions

1) What are some scriptural metaphors (symbols) that we use? 1 Sam. 16:13; Hosea 6:1-3; Mt 26:26-28; Luke 5:35-37; Acts 2:13-17._____
_____
_____
_____

2) What are some metaphors that we use in our culture now?_____
_____
_____
_____

Prophecy Visions & Dreams

3) a. What kind of vision is found in Luke 1:10-24?____

   b. What kind of vision is found in Acts 11:5-6? Acts 16: 9-10?____

4) a. What is a night vision? Daniel 2:19.____

   b. Soul dream? Jer. 23: 25-27.____

   c. False dream? Job 4:12-21.____

5) What are some of the things God calls us to do to gain revelation if we receive a metaphoric dream? Gen. 40:8-12; Daniel 2:1-19; Daniel 9:3-23; Daniel 10:2-14.___

6) What are some symbols that might be used in a dream and what are their typical meanings?____

The Speaking Prophet
Chapter 8

In the Old Testament, the Word of the Lord was also given by the speaking prophet. Generally, this indicated that a prophet did not see a picture but was speaking to the people or individual by the Spirit of the Lord. They either heard the word or voiced the word that came to them. In describing this type of activity, the phrase frequently used in the Bible is, "the Word of the Lord came to so and so." In the first book of Samuel, [39] we see that the Lord spoke to Samuel, who did not see a picture but heard the voice of the Lord call him. Later in that same passage, we see the Lord revealed His thoughts to Samuel regarding Eli. In II Samuel 7:4 we see Nathan the prophet heard the word of the Lord regarding David's sin. The term used is, "the Lord said." We learn from these scriptures that the Lord spoke to and through prophets as well as giving them pictures.

Sometimes it appears the Word of the Lord was given spontaneously. In II Kings 20:1-7, Isaiah prophesied to King Hezekiah about his imminent death. Hezekiah responded to this word with a petition for healing instead of death. As a result, God responded to Hezekiah. Before Isaiah stepped out of the castle, he spontaneously received a word of prophecy for Hezekiah regarding his healing.[40]

Hearing the voice of the Lord can come in two ways. It may come as a message ahead of time, or spontaneous in the moment. When it comes ahead of time, it is given by revelation to the person's mind. The prophet knows most of what is going to be said before the time of release. These messages may also come while reading the scriptures. A thought may suddenly come to mind that a particular scripture should be given to a person or group. When these messages are received, the person is prepared mentally and emotionally to release the subject matter. It is revelatory in that the person receives the message to his intellectual mind. Messages of this kind are most easy to write down so they can be given later or relayed at a gathering where the guidelines do not allow for spontaneous release of a prophetic word.

Another way a prophetic word may come is through the spirit. The person giving the word does not know the message of the Lord until after it is spoken and subsequently heard. These messages are often an interpretation of the Gift of Tongues or a spontaneous prophetic utterance. The person may receive an initial phrase but must step out in faith, believing God for the rest as it is released as one speaks. The Holy Spirit uses the person's tongue and voice. These messages are revelatory in that they bring revelation to those listening, including the one speaking the message. Often these prophetic releases are given in the moment and have a timing aspect to them. For example, a few years back, my church had a project for outreach, and they were presenting the details to the congregation to get everyone on board for the finances. There was a little hesitation among the congregation to take on another financial burden unless it had the Lord's approval. There was a spontaneous prophetic message given at the meeting that conveyed the Lord's approval and intent to back the project, which brought a unanimous desire from the congregation to support it. The message given needed to be given at that time because everyone who needed to hear it was there for the vote. I believe if the message had been held or given at a later time, it would not have had the effect it did in the moment. Timing had a lot to do with the outcome.

Commonly the way the Lord speaks to us varies with each individual. Most of us will experience hearing His voice, seeing pictures in our minds eye, getting a spiritual impression, or having the scripture highlighted to us. We are not limited to one particular way the Lord speaks to us, just like it is in our other relationships. Sometimes we text, phone, email, write notes, send pictures, or speak face to face with our loved ones and friends.

These examples are only guidelines for how the

Holy Spirit may communicate His plans to His people through a prophetic message. Remember, most importantly is that however the Holy Spirit chooses to speak to us, He intends to have a relationship with us and then for us to have a relationship with others. This is the core motivation behind having the God of all creation speak to us and for us to hear his voice. Jesus said in John 10:27, "my sheep hear my voice, and I know them, and they follow me."

The Speaking Prophet Study Questions

1) What do we mean when we say, "I heard the voice of the Lord?" 1 Sam. 3:1-10; 2 Kings 20:1-7; Acts 9:4.____

_____
_____
_____
_____

2) What is the difference between a spontaneous word and a word given to the intellect? 2 Kings 20 1-7._____

_____
_____
_____
_____

3) Does the person hearing God's voice always know what will be said prior to release? Explain.
2 Kings 20 1-7._____
_____
_____
_____

4) How may timing for the release of a message affect the outcome?_____
_____
_____
_____

5) Name some of the varied ways the Lord may speak to us?_____
_____
_____
_____
_____

6) Name some of the ways the speaking prophet can deliver a word._____
_____
_____
_____

Fasting and Worship
Chapter 9

Anytime we talk about hearing, we must also include ways to quiet our souls to enable our spiritual ears to hear. Two spiritual disciplines are fasting, and worship which are invaluable for cultivating a quiet, listening heart. Fasting is one of the ways the spirit is sensitized to the Lord's voice. When we fast, we humble ourselves before the Lord to gain revelation and wisdom for God's mind and will, for specific guidance in our lives. We see this with Daniel, who had a vision of the future and was given the interpretation after twenty-one days of fasting.[41] We can also fast for breakthrough in a circumstance or victory over the enemy. This kind of fast is absolutely part of the Christian walk. Jesus said in Mathew 17:21 that a particular demon could not go out of a person except by prayer and fasting.[42] This story in scripture teaches us that fasting has the power to defeat the enemy and increase our faith. We may do this kind of fast individually or corporately. On the corporate level, these fasts are usually done to gain victory for certain critical issues in the local church, or in our world system and governing laws. Often the Lord will give spiritual strategy and clues as to some of the obstacles that could be hindering breakthrough. These strategies and clues are a form of prophetic knowledge given for intercession and discernment to reveal thrones of iniquity and redeeming qualities.

However, I believe that sometimes, the Lord would have us fast just to hear His voice and find out what is on His mind. To fast humbly to receive more of His presence is what I believe Jesus was talking about in Mathew when He said:

> "Can the children of the bridechamber mourn, as long as the bridegroom is with them? But the days will come when the bridegroom shall be taken from them, and then shall they fast." (Mathew 9:15).

In the previous passage, the Lord speaks of the day His disciples would mourn for Him. This word in the Greek *(pentheo)* which means to lament for a person much the same way one would lament for someone who had gone on a long journey or had died. As His disciples, we still need to long for His presence and listen for His voice. Quieting ourselves through fasting and prayer is one of the ways we can do that. It can easily be said fasting is another one of the ways we've been given to worship the Lord

Singing and declaring praise and worship is another way we are sensitized to hear His voice. In the natural, when we focus on an object, our senses become alert to changes and activities relating to that object. We often block out other sounds to pay particular attention to what we are focused on. This is what happens when we focus on the Lord. Our hearing and spiritual sight become keener as we block out the distractions around us, allowing us to have more fine-tuned hearing to the Lord's voice. The Lord also enjoys the praises of His people both corporately and individually as we demonstrate our awe of Him and place ourselves in a posture of worship and reception. He often releases revelation to us during this time. When little children want to be picked up by their daddy, they will often lift their hands in a gesture of desire and open reception. In response, daddies with pleasure will scoop their little ones up into their arms, revealing their tender love for them. I believe the same is true with us, and our Father in heaven. When we lift our hands in praise and worship in that same gesture, He scoops us up in the spirit, so to speak and tenderly reveals His love and heart to us.

When Elisha was asked by the wicked king Joram to prophesy instructions about war, Elisha asked for a harp player to come and play. When the sound of music began, the word of the Lord came to Elisha, and he was able to speak to the king what the Lord had in mind for the war. I'm sure it wasn't just any music but probably a sound to the Lord because Elisha was a prophet for God.[43] Elisha was familiar with the connection of hearing God and music, especially the harp, from the experiences of those who had gone before him. When Samuel the prophet was working with Saul, he sent him to a group of Saul's student prophets where he would receive the anointing to become king.[44] These prophets were playing harps, tambourines, and lyres, while they were prophesying to Saul, who under that musical sound and anointing, prophesied with them and then was changed into a new man. Later, when Saul had been disobedient to God, an evil spirit came on him. A servant of Saul's suggested David, as someone who could play the harp for Saul so that the evil spirit would leave him[45]. Praise with music was a part of hearing the Lord's heart and relieving people from darkness back then, and I believe still is one of the ways we hear His voice now.

It is also written in Psalm 22:2 that God inhabits or is enthroned in the praises of His people. As we praise Him, He responds with His weighty presence and power often with breakthrough for us on a personal and group level. I know many who have been healed and found freedom during worship as He responds to us when we honor His name. He will always reveal Himself to us by the written word. But He still reveals Himself to His people through many of the ways He revealed Himself to those who are written about in scripture. As Paul and Silas were praising the Lord in prison after being beaten, the prison was shaken by an earthquake, and the doors of their cell were opened. God showed up and revealed Himself as the ultimate authority in their praises, leading to great revelation for salvation to the prison guard.[46]

Fasting and Worship Study Questions

1) What do we mean by the term spiritual disciplines?
_____
_____
_____
_____
_____

2) What are some reasons why it is important to fast? Daniel 10:2,12; Mathew 21:17; Mark 9:29._____
_____
_____
_____
_____

3) What did Jesus mean when He spoke about fasting for the bridegroom? Mathew 9:15. _____
_____
_____
_____
_____
_____

4) How does worship and praise assist us in hearing the Lord's voice?_____
_____
_____
_____
_____
_____

5) What do the accounts of King Saul's tormenting evil spirit and Paul and Silas in prison have in common?___
_____
_____
_____
_____

A Word in Due Season
Chapter 10

In the early 1900's, a new doctrine began to take formal structure that would try to refute the ever-increasing movement of the manifestational gifts of the Holy Spirit. This theology came to be known as Cessation of the Gifts.[47] This idea essentially declared that the manifestational gifts of the Holy Spirit found in the book of Acts and I Corinthians 12 & 14, had ceased when the Canon (the Bible) was complete. The intent of this theology was developed to destroy the fresh Holy Spirit initiated Pentecostal movement that was coming out of the Azusa Street revival in 1906. Since those who held to this doctrine had not had an experience with the supernatural manifestational gifts of the Holy Spirit, they decided they were no longer needed or valid. As a result, many missed the strength and supernatural help these gifts give to the Body of Christ. However, the Holy Spirit continued to sweep His people with revelation and openness to His activity. Today the Spirit-filled facet of the Body of

Christ is the fastest growing globally. The prophetic anointing has become a valid presence in the church and sincerely needed for the stability that it brings. So, what does this gift do for us? Perhaps looking at the needs will help us see the fruit of this gift.

In II Samuel 12:1-13 Nathan, the prophet is used as a plumb line in David's life to expose sin. The word of the Lord caused David to repent and then to redirect and draw close to the Lord. The prophetic anointing is used today in the same way. When sin is hidden, it has the power to continue, but when it is exposed, it often produces repentance. Some hidden sin can only be exposed by supernatural means because humankind is so skillful at hiding evil. God, in His grace, will often send a prophet to one of his children to expose sin privately in an attitude of protection before He exposes publicly. When prophetic words expose sin, the person sent must never come in an attitude of judgment. The judging heart says, "I could never do that." To be judged by another causes a person to recoil rather than to draw near. It also demonstrates an attitude of pride on the part of the person prophesying. Paul said in his letter to the Galatians that we should walk in meekness:

> "Brethren, if a man be overtaken in a fault, ye which are spiritual, restore such an one in the spirit of meekness; considering thyself, lest thou also be tempted." (Gal. 6:1). (KJV)

It is important to maintain an attitude of meekness and humility when giving a prophetic word to someone.

Another purpose for releasing a prophetic word is related to support. We often need promises and prophetic promptings from the Lord to keep us moving in the right direction and toward the call that God has for us. We may have had a promise or vision that took time before it was fulfilled. Circumstances arise that discourage us and destroy our hope. Prophetic words spoken into our lives restore our hope and increase our faith, causing us to stand firm in difficult places. A few years ago, I was diagnosed with cancer. Just before my diagnosis, I was given Isaiah 41:10 by several different people. It declares:

> "Fear not for I am with you. Be not dismayed, for I am Your God. I will strengthen you to difficulties. I will help You and I will uphold you with my victorious right hand of righteousness and justice." (Isaiah 41:10). [48]

This scripture was given to me seven times by several different people. When I was going through chemotherapy and radiation and facing possible death, this scripture was a prophetic word given to keep my faith up and my heart firm. The prophetic word of the Lord literally upheld me during difficult times.

God is an all-knowing God who will give us prophetic words or visions and dreams to guide us. He directs us to keep moving in the right direction but also warns us of impending danger or struggle ahead.

These warnings come so that we will stop what we are about to do or pray to avert the plans of the enemy.

When I was younger, the Lord had directed me to begin an Aglow women's group in my town. The prophetic word came as a dream to me. I began moving in that direction about two and a half years later. I had a prayer gathering at my house one morning and had decided earlier that I would start planning the first meeting after the prayer gathering ended. I was going to ask a singing group in my area to perform for the first meeting. When I was about to step out of my door, a friend of mine rang the bell. When I opened the door, she declared a prophetic warning to me. She said she was out doing her own business when the Lord told her to go to my house and that it was an emergency. When she arrived, she declared to me, "The Lord says, Stand still and do not move." This word was a warning that gave me direction and demanded my obedience. It was a few months later that I was diagnosed with cancer. It would have been very difficult to start a new Aglow

Chapter with the struggles I had to deal with during treatment. Once I was done and healed, the Lord led me to start the Aglow at the right time.

When the warning comes as a strategy to avert evil, we are to give ourselves to prayer for that cause. God trusts us with His plans and lets us know ahead of time what they are. This is one of His strategies for thwarting the devil's plans. Many of us hear the prophets of today blow the trumpet to call the troops for warfare prayer corporately. Global prophets like Chuck Pierce, Cindy Jacobs, and many others send out calls to prayer after receiving warning from the Lord. Many times the plans of the enemy are rendered impotent because of the unified prayers of the saints.

Part of the prophetic anointing includes testifying about Jesus. Jesus said in Revelation that testifying about Him is prophetic:

> "For the testimony of Jesus Christ is the spirit of prophecy."(Revelation 19:10).

We declare under this anointing who Jesus is and what He did for humanity. If we study the ministry of Jesus while He walked the earth, we can see that all He did was to reach those separated from Him by using every means possible, including the supernatural. The Holy Spirit is the spirit of prophecy whose desire it is to help us fulfill the Great Commission command to go into all the world and preach the gospel and make disciples. Prophesying to the lost to impart a hunger to them for Christ is included in the gift. God reaches into the hearts of men by speaking into their lives even before they know or have a revelation of Him. We see this with people like Nebuchadnezzar, a pagan king with a God-given dream, or Samuel, a boy prophet who heard the Lord before he knew Him. We must be ready and sensitive to the voice of the Lord when He wants to use us to speak to unbelievers prophetically.

A Word In Due Season Study Questions

1) What is the theology of Cessation of the Gifts?_____
_____
_____
_____

2) What did Cessation of the Gifts try to do and describe how is it still operating in churches today?____
_____
_____
_____
_____

3) How does the prophetic word support individuals in their daily life?_____
_____
_____
_____
_____

4) What is one of the ways the prophetic word is used to keep the Body of Christ in alignment with the standard and agenda of the Lord?_____
_____
_____
_____

5) How is the prophetic word used in to help people when there is a lack of hope?_____
_____
_____

Manifestations
Chapter 11

When the Holy Spirit came upon people in the both the Old and New Testaments, they displayed many different physical manifestations. The same Holy Spirit that dwelt in Jesus and produced the spontaneous, explosive release of life that raised Him from the dead dwells in us. This livening or quickening of our bodies can be very powerful. In the human body, Adenosine Triphosphate is the energy that is released in every cell to cause it to produce all of the electrical activities that must happen to do what it has to do. Thousands of little explosions happen every day in our bodies. The Holy Spirit's explosive life-giving power is multiplied many times this little bit of power that keeps our bodies working. In Acts 1:8, this power in the Greek is called "dunamis."

The English word for dynamite is derived from this word in the Greek. When the Holy Spirit releases His power to us, we often respond with different manifestations. These may appear strange to someone who is not familiar with these activities. However, in Acts 2, we see those who were watching the Holy Spirit's power moving on the disciples concluded that they were drunk. On other occasions, we see those who were under the weighty presence of the Lord fell on their faces. [49] They trembled and shook [50] and became weak and unable to stand. [51] Their tongues stuck to the roof of their mouths,[52] and they fell into trance-like states.[53] Some other manifestations that might appear may be, a thumping heart, breathlessness, feelings of urgency, jolts and jerks, feeling heat or fire, trembling hands, and other manifestations that indicate the presence of the Holy Spirit. I believe these are our body's responses to a very powerful, holy God. When His Spirit comes upon us, sometimes we cannot help but respond out of our lowly state as humans.

    The word for the Lord's glory in Hebrew is qabod (קבוד). This word means heavy or weightiness. It implies that sometimes when the Lord's presence by

His Spirit falls upon a person, they may respond to the weight of it. In II Chronicles 5:14, we see when the Lord's glory filled the house, the priests could not stand to minister. The weight of His glory caused them to fall on their faces. Manifestations or symptoms of the presence of the Holy Spirit are a normal part of moving under His power and should be accepted. However, sometimes, people may begin moving in the flesh and producing manifestations to obtain notice. These activities reflect poorly on the genuine presence of the Lord. We must be careful not to exaggerate these manifestations because it steals the glory and focus from the Lord and puts it on us. I doubt the Lord takes any pleasure in being robbed of His glory.

MANIFESTATIONS STUDY QUESTIONS

1) What is the explosive energy of the Holy Spirit called? Luke 24:49; Acts 1:8. _____

2) What are some activities that we see that are manifestations of the Holy Spirit? Acts 2:4; Acts 7:32; Acts 9:4; Daniel 10:8; Acts 10:10. _____

3) How can the manifestations of the Holy Spirit become perverted? _____

4) How do false manifestations affect the Body of Christ? _____

Proper Prophetic Release Chapter 12

When we study Jesus' managing skills in the scripture, we see that He is a very kind but firm manager of people. In Revelation 2:1-3:22, we learn that Jesus most often addressed the churches with what they had been doing well before addressing how they could improve. When He corrects, his motivation is to draw people to repentance and toward Him. Because God is love, all His activities are motivated by His love for people. In Ezekiel 18:23, God said that it is not His pleasure that the wicked should perish but that they turn from their ways and live. The motivation and heart of love will always be present in the prophetic word of His Spirit. When we release a corrective, prophetic word to an individual or the corporate body, there should always be room for grace that leads to repentance. Our judgments and attitudes about certain situations are better kept to ourselves and dealt with before the Lord.

Prophecy should never be something that comes from the soul or personal experience, but must always come from the heart of God. Some are so taken with what God is teaching them in their own lives that they try to make everyone else learn the same thing by using prophetic means. What is said might be a good teaching but should not be passed off as a prophecy if it is not. Only that which comes from the Holy Spirit as a prophetic word in our inner man should be given as prophecy. Otherwise, we are tainting the gift.

When a prophetic word is released with the prophet as the source rather than God as the source, it interferes with the focus of the hearer. Preceding the prophetic word with, "the Lord told me to tell you," causes the attention to turn toward the speaker rather than the Lord. It is more beneficial to say something like, "I believe the Lord is saying." This way, the attention of the hearer is to the Lord rather than to the prophet. That is not to say that there aren't times one might say, "I am sensing a word for you," or "I feel the Lord showed me something." which can be said in conversation. However, at the point of release, it is better to take the focus off our ability to hear the Lord and to place it on the person hearing the message; this causes the hearer to focus on the Lord rather than the prophet. The prophetic word from the Holy Spirit will validate to the hearers that it is something supernatural because it will witness to them or speak to circumstances in his or her life. This form of release often supports and encourages the person's or group's hearing, to continue or move forward in faith.

Another difficulty is our desire to be in control. Trying to be in control happens in part because we do not like to feel insecure or vulnerable. Being in control makes us feel safe. When a Word is released, we should recognize that God has control as to how and when it turns out. Our feelings of vulnerability may cause us to try to make the prophetic word we released happen on our terms. We may try to manipulate the timing and the circumstances to force the word to come true sooner than it was supposed to or happen the way we think it should. Forcing a word produces the fruit of frustration and anger for the person releasing the word and for those who have heard the word. The recipients then feel like they have been pushed around spiritually. Letting go of the responsibility for the outcome of a prophetic word is the best way to handle the need to control. Once a word is released to a person, ownership of the word should be released, as well. The Holy Spirit is the one who owns the word. After all, it originated with Him. He has the legal right to cause it to happen in His time and His way. Sometimes the need to control will play havoc with one's attitude in the area of pride and position. When a person is used to having leaders respond to their specific prophetic words, pride can become an issue. The prophet may begin to assume their prophetic words place them in a position of authority over the leaders. They may begin to dictate and try to control the direction and trajectory of the leadership's vision. The keywords here are control and pride. When this happens, the leadership begins to feel like they are being manipulated to think a certain way. This attitude must be extinguished either by personal repentance or addressed by the leadership if it continues. If it is not dealt with by leadership, the church will suffer division and lack of growth.

Humbly walking in the prophetic anointing is the safest place for a believer to be. Trying to take credit for words that have been spoken in the past only reveals a deeper issue of the need to be recognized, perhaps related to insecurity. In the book of Mathew, when people were offended at Jesus anointing, he said:

> "A prophet is not without honor except in his own country and among his own people." (Mathew 13:57b).

From this verse, we see that there is an element of honor given to a prophet. This honor comes from those who have received a word, which has encouraged and protected those who have heard. Honor comes from those who speak about another rather than those who speak about themselves. When a word has been given, most will remember who released it. The prophet doesn't need to remind everyone who said it because God is the One Who really said it. The most important thing is that the word was released to accomplish change or bring hope to hearts.

PROPER PROPHETIC RELEASE STUDY QUESTIONS

1) What is the foundation for proper prophetic release? Give an example. 1 Corinthian 13; 1 John 4:2, 7-21._____
_____
_____

2) What would be the proper way to notify someone you have a prophetic word for them?_____
_____
_____
_____

3) Where should the focus of a prophetic word be?_
_____
_____
_____
_____

4) How does a controlling personality affect the result of a prophetic word? _____

_____
_____
_____
_____

5) What does the passage that Jesus spoke in Mathew 13:57 imply? _____

_____
_____
_____

6) How does honor relate to promoting oneself in prophetic ministry? _____

_____
_____
_____

False Prophets
Chapter 13

Standards for false prophets have been written down in Scripture for our use and protection. However, any single test is not sufficient for deciding truth or error. We must use more than one criterion for identifying a false prophet. Looking at the fruit of the life as well as the fruit of the word given is a necessary part of testing a word. Enlisting the gift of Discerning of Spirits also aids us in determining truth. In Deuteronomy it talks about this:

> "If there arises among you a prophet or a dreamer of dreams and he gives you a sign or a wonder, and the sign or the wonder comes to pass, of which he spoke to you, saying, 'Let us go after other gods'-which you have not known-and let us serve them, you shall not listen to the words of that prophet or that dreamer of dreams, for the Lord your God is testing you to know

whether you love the Lord your God with all your heart and with all your soul." (Deuteronomy 13:1-4).

In this passage, God is speaking about a false prophet whose prophecy had come true. But, the test for a genuine word from the Lord was not if it came true or if it was accurate but its fruit. It was if the prophet's word led one toward the Lord rather than away from Him. In Deuteronomy, the Lord spoke about another prophetic test:

"When a prophet speaks in the name of the Lord, if the thing does not happen or come to pass that is the thing which the Lord has not spoken; the prophet has spoken it presumptuously; you shall not be afraid of him." (Deuteronomy 18:22).

In this passage, the Lord explains that when a prophet speaks, and the word does not come to pass, that prophet's word is not from the Lord but has spoken a word presumptuously. This verse is often used to determine if a prophet speaking today is a true prophet or a false prophet. The difficulty with using this single verse as a standard is related to the timing of the fulfillment of the prophetic word. Many of the prophets of old, like Ezekiel, Isaiah and others, spoke words to their people that eventually came true. However, some of their words are yet to be fulfilled especially the messianic scriptures and those relating to the Jewish people today. If the people who lived in the days of the prophets used this verse as their only criterion for true prophets, Ezekiel, Isaiah, John the Apostle, and others would have been labeled false prophets. Much of what they prophesied came true many years after they were dead and gone. Some of their words still have not been fulfilled today.

John gives us a guideline in I John 4:2. He tells us to test the spirits. Every spirit that does not confess that Jesus Christ has come in the flesh is not of God. I believe He is speaking here of the confession that Jesus Christ is the sacrificial lamb and Son of God who was physically present. A spirit of Antichrist would never confess the Savior of the world. This test can be joined with others to help us discern when a prophet speaks. One of the best tests to determine genuine prophetic anointing is in Mathew's gospel where Jesus spoke concerning false prophets:

> "Beware of false prophets, who come to you in sheep's clothing, but inwardly they are ravenous wolves. "<u>You will know them by their fruits</u>. Do men gather grapes from thorn bushes or figs from thistles?" (Mathew 7:15, 16a).

I do not believe Jesus is speaking of human frailty here. If that were the case, no one could move under the anointing of the Holy Spirit, whether prophesying or preaching. I believe he is speaking of a consistent release of bad fruit that causes dissension, disunity, pride, and misalignment with the scripture that leads one away from the Truth. When hearing, we must ask ourselves questions that help us evaluate. That is not to say that every time a prophetic speaks, we must treat it with a critical or suspicious attitude. I don't want to negate the supernatural discerning work of the Holy Spirit. Many times a word given is readily accepted because it receives the confirming witness of the Holy Spirit within us. However, when a prophetic word declares something new, or when it doesn't seem to fit just right, we become as responsible for receiving a prophetic word as we have been for releasing a word. Mentally asking a few safety questions will help. Does it produce good fruit? Does it ring true with the heart and word of Scripture? Do others in the Body of Christ witness to it? Is the prophet established by the truth of the word released? Does it move the listener closer to the Lord or salvation? What do others in the Body sense about the word, and has God confirmed it? These questions can aid us when a word may come that may not be confirming something we already have in our heart.

When Satan tested Eve in the garden, he twisted just a few words of God's command about the tree.

When Jesus was in the wilderness under the same test, Satan quoted scripture perfectly to entice Jesus to fail. The Scripture teaches us that Satan comes as an angel of light to deceive and seduce. He attempts to lead us away from Jesus. As we walk in the Spirit, we need to consider and remember these warnings Jesus gave us. We must not be ignorant of the devil's devises.

Another wise approach when receiving a word is to make sure we do not superimpose our interpretation and theology upon it. Too many times, the prophetic word has come under suspicion even though it is consistent with the spirit and standard of Scripture because someone placed their own timing or interpretation on what the Lord was saying. The religious leaders of Jesus' day did this very thing. They were expecting a king who would rescue Israel in the natural. They decided Jesus could not be the Messiah because He did not fit their interpretation of the prophetic scriptures of the Old Testament. When giving and receiving a word from the Lord, God's timing and interpretation is important.

In Revelation, Jesus declares:

> "Behold, I am coming quickly! Blessed is he who keeps the words of the prophecy of this book." (Revelation 22:7).

John could have interpreted the words "I am coming quickly" to mean within a year, five years from then or longer. Who would have thought that Christ's idea of quickly would be longer than two thousand years? As was said before, sometimes we decide what the Lord is talking about without waiting for Him to let us know what He means. The disciples did this when our Lord was warning them about being aware of the leaven of the Sadducees and Pharisees. He was talking about the religious leaders' doctrine, but the disciples thought He was talking about needing to have brought bread.[54] Sometimes this happens when He speaks to us today. We apply our interpretation to a word, and when it doesn't turn out as we expect, we decide it was not from the Lord. When the Lord speaks to us through a prophet or to our spirit, it is wise to wait for understanding or repeat just what was said and not add our little twist on it.

False Prophets Study Questions

1) What are some of the criteria to determine false prophesy? Deut.13:1-4; 18:22; 1 John 4:2-3; Mathew 7:15-20._____
_____
_____
_____
_____
_____

2) How does the gift of Discerning of Spirits help with false prophesy? 1 John 4:1._____
_____
_____
_____
_____

3) Is a prophetic word necessarily true if it has scripture within it? Explain. Genesis 3:1-6; Mathew 4:1-11._____
_____
_____
_____

4) How can we misinterpret a prophetic word even though it seems clear? How? Rev.22:7; Mathew 16:5-12._____
_____
_____

Jezebel Activity
Chapter 14

In his time, Elijah was established as a man of God and a great prophet. However, his prophetic ministry occurred during a most difficult time for any prophet. Israel was led astray under King Ahab's reign and Queen Jezebel's supernaturally, manipulative, idolatrous ways. Elijah acted as a plumb line and apostolic prophet to the nation. He called the people back to God and spoke harsh words to the King and Queen. Of course, this brought the ire of the Queen. Jezebel desired power and authority over the Hebrew nation, and Elijah consistently stepped in her way. He had the God-given power of the Holy Spirit to cause obstacles to rise against her. As a result, she desired to destroy the true prophet of the Lord and the true leadership of the king. She worshipped Baal, a pagan deity and Asherah, his female counterpart. These gods were related to the sun as lord of the day and fertility. The name Baal means "lord" or "master." Asherim were wooden poles that were in the shape of an idol and planted in the ground forming a grove. Asherah was associated with a very sensual goddess. Many of the religious rituals performed for worship of these gods included cult prostitution and sexual orgies. The worship of these gods was of the basest form of religious ritual. We see in I Kings 18:25-29 that the priests of Baal practiced bloodletting. They would cut themselves with knives and sticks as a sacrifice to gain favor from Baal.

Jezebel practiced witchcraft, which utilizes dark supernatural means for personal gain. King Ahab was bound to her by his lustful soul. He was a self-centered, spoiled man who let Jezebel lead him into evil because he stood to gain whatever he wanted. He built a grove in the high place for the Israelites to worship, and he allowed her to kill the prophets of God without blinking an eye. Although it does not say, I wonder what kind of sexual rituals he encountered in his worship in the Asherah groves. Ahab was by no means an innocent bystander, seduced into following a wicked woman. He allowed her to run the kingdom.

The name Jezebel has at least three possible meanings: Baal exalts, Baal is husband of, or unchaste. Whatever her name means, Jezebel fits all three. We must remember that she was a worshiper of both Baal and Ashtoreth. Often when idols are worshipped, demonic spirits begin taking possession of those who open themselves up to pagan worship. In 1 Corinthians 10: 19-21, Paul teaches that idols are nothing but wood and stone, but what the people worshipped were the devils behind the idols.

When we look at Jezebel, we must see the spirit behind her. This devil with evil power influenced her and used her to accomplish his evil plans. Jezebel was a willing participant and took pleasure in this ungodly alliance. However, Jezebel, the woman perished, but the spirit behind Jezebel still operates today. This spirit is neither male nor female and is indiscriminate in the vessel it will use. When a person operates under this devil's influence, they will manifest many of the same characteristics that Jezebel displayed. That is why many call this the spirit of Jezebel. It isn't

Jezebel but the demon behind the ancient woman. This demonic influence is still at work, trying to prevent the true prophetic voice from going forth to accomplish the purposes of God.

Because this deity stood for fertility, we can expect an attack on the reproductive, fruitfulness, and fertility of the Lord's Kingdom. The Body of Christ, local churches, and any other para-church ministry that is related to multiplication can be hindered. If not dealt with, this spirit will render the ministry impotent and barren. The apostolic, prophetic, and pastoral leaders are often pounded with intimidation by this dominant, controlling personality. It often threatens to cause trouble or threatens the wrath of God for disobedience to its prophetic words. These Jezebel sufferers are often accurate prophetically, which initially lends legitimacy to their words. But this prophetic accuracy is then used later to intimidate into submission. That is why it is so necessary to pay attention to fruit, as well as accuracy. This voice often gains a following and begins causing division among brothers and sisters. It tries to gain favor and power to lead the people after its agenda. If the leaders do not submit to the word of this false prophet, this spirit will begin attacking the leadership's integrity and spirituality, sowing discord in the body. That is what happened to Elijah as he stood against unrighteousness. Ahab had the nerve to declare that Elijah was the reason for all the trouble in Israel.[55] This spirit will also use manipulation and enticement to gain power and control, usurping the place of authority. When Ahab desired Naboth's vineyard, he allowed Jezebel to use whatever means she had to gain it. We see that she used fasting, deception, and manipulation, even enlisting others to do her dirty work. It's interesting to note that the name Naboth means fruit. He also owned a vineyard, which produced grape juice and wine. In the Old Testament, wine often symbolized the Holy Spirit. In Jezebel's pagan worship, vegetables were a part of offerings to the pagan gods. Ahab wanted Naboth's vineyard for a vegetable garden. When the Jezebel spirit is operating, we will often see an attempt to steal the fruit of the vineyard of the Lord and make it into a garden that produces for ungodliness. This activity quenches the true release of the Holy Spirit, who is symbolically known as the new wine. This spirit also has a supernatural power to entice. It taps into a small desire in the soul. As true people and prophets of God, we must continually evaluate our plans and desires, to prevent this spirit from gaining influence over our behavior. King Ahab allowed Jezebel to incite him to do evil because there was a place in his heart that desired the things she could get for him. We see this implied in 1 Kings 21:25 which states:

> "But there was none like unto Ahab,
> which did sell himself to work wickedness
> in the sight of the LORD, whom Jezebel
> his wife stirred up." (1 Kings 21:25). (KJV).

Ahab did not realize he exchanged his fruitfulness and prosperity in the Lord for a few glass baubles. Jezebel rendered him impotent. He became one of her eunuchs, losing his authority and kingly power to her. The word "stirred up" in this verse is the Hebrew word

Cuwth. This word means to incite, allure, instigate, and entice. Since Jezebel was practicing witchcraft, there is little doubt she had a supernatural, ungodly anointing to influence those around her. When Jehu came to destroy Jezebel, he asked the eunuchs who were with her, but on his side, to throw her down, which they did promptly. Jehu's name means Yah Is. Symbolically as the all-existent God and a type of Christ, Jehu came for Jezebel, but the eunuchs had to throw her down before he could destroy her. If we have been influenced and enticed by this spirit, either by allowing this spirit control over us through a relationship or by submitting to its spiritual control, then we need to repent and throw down all association with it. Opening ourselves to the cleansing power of the all-existent Christ will eliminate this influence from our lives.

As we move in the prophetic anointing, we need to be ever throwing down anything that even begins to look like Jezebel. In Revelation 2:20, Jesus rebuked the church of Thyatira for tolerating the woman

Jezebel and allowing her to continue to seduce and deceive the flock. Interestingly enough, she must have had a prophetic anointing that had some accuracy because the people were tolerating her deceptive ways. She even called herself a prophetess and had a group of people who were following her powers of influence. Jesus Himself dealt with this Jezebel by sending a sickness to her because she would not repent. That must have been an extremely serious offense because we see the Great Physician do the opposite and send sickness to stop the perpetuation of evil. It is to our advantage to be on the alert for any signs of this spirit's activity. Eventually, the true prophetic voice will expose this spirit for what it is, breaking open the way to get rid of it.

John's revelatory vision of Jesus in the book of Revelation is the very thing that exposed Jezebel in the church at Thyatira. The revelatory work of the Holy Spirit is still operative today. If we humbly allow Him to check our hearts to see if there are any remnants of a Jezebel or Ahab like personality, He will most certainly reveal it to us so we can repent and renounce it. As the sons and daughters of God, we need to be done with this spirit and move on in the prophetic power and anointing that God has released to us to accomplish the Great Commission, in our families, our towns, cities, and nations.

Jezebel Study Questions

1) What are some characteristics and personality traits of Jezebel in the Bible? 1 Kings 18:4; 19:1-3; 21:2-15, 25; 2 Kings 9:30; Rev. 2:20-23. _____
_____
_____
_____

2) Who or what did Jezebel worship? 1 Kings 16:31; 18:19; 1 Corinthians 10:19-20. _____
_____
_____

3) What did her influence try to accomplish with Ahab and the people of Israel? 1 Kings 18:17-18; 21:20-26. ___
_____
_____
_____

4) Was Jezebel's influence possibly supernatural? 1 Kings 21:9; 9:22; Revelation 2:20-23.___If so, then from where did her power come? 2 Kings 9:22; 2 Chron. 33:6._____

_____
_____
_____

5) What is one especially prominent tactic that Jezebel used to get her way? 1 Kings 19:2-4._____

_____
_____
_____

6) When we say Jezebel spirit, what are we speaking about?_____

_____
_____
_____
_____

7) How does the Jezebel spirit influence leadership? 1 Kings 21:5-8; Rev. 2:20-23. _____

_____
_____
_____

8) What would be some personality traits that would help leaders recognize this deceptive spirit? 1 Kings 19:2-3; 2 Kings 9:30-31; Rev. 2:20._____

_____
_____
_____
_____

9) What is the consequence of allowing this spirit to operate? 1 Kings 21:22; Revelations 2:18-23. _____
_____
_____
_____

10) What can we do to rid ourselves of this influence? 2 Kings 9:32-35; Revelation 2:21. _____
_____
_____
_____

What will Christ do in this process?
2 Kings 9: 33; Rev. 2:22._____
_____
_____
_____

11) What should our heart attitude always be as we move prophetically? Mathew 15:17-20; 1 Corinthians 13; 14:1; James 4:6-10; 3:8-12; Gal. 5:22-26._____
_____

Conclusion
Chapter 15

As we move in the prophetic anointing God has given us, let us always be alert and mindful of some of the potholes into which we can fall. Let us also be intensely aware of the prophetic God we serve, who created us to be prophetic people to declare His purposes to the ends of the earth. He has given us the Holy Scriptures and His own Holy Spirit of power to declare His voice so humankind may know what He has to say and that He came to save them. He has also given us the prophetic anointing for our reinforcement so we won't faint or get weary in doing His will. We are a great and privileged people because we serve the only God in all creation Who has a very intricate, living, intimate, loving, personal relationship with His people.

Notes: All Scriptural references are New King James Version unless otherwise noted.

[1] Joel 2:28 And it shall come to pass afterward That I will pour out My Spirit on all flesh; Your sons and your daughters shall prophesy, Your old men shall dream dreams, Your young men shall see visions.

[2] Ac 2:15, 16 "For these are not drunk, as you suppose, since it is only the third hour of the day. But this is what was spoken by the prophet Joel:

[3] M.G. Easton, *Easton's Bible Dictionary*, (CM 1897) Prophet

[4] 2 Samuel 7:2-17; 1 Kings 22:5-7; 2 Kings 19:1-35; Judges 4:4-10

[5] 2 Chronicles 15:1-8; 2 Kings 6:1-7; 1 Kings 17:8-24; 1 Samuel 3:3-18
Jonah 3:2-10; Ezekiel 2:3-8; Philippians 3:13-17; James 5:10

[6] Isaiah 61:1; Luke 4:18

[7] John 4:9-28; 39-42

[8] Lawrence, O Richards, *Richards Complete Bible Dictionary* (World Bible Publishers, Inc, IA, 2002), p. 510

[9] Strong's Concordance of the Hebrew and Greek, ajrchv Arche Word Origin: Greek, Noun Feminine, Strong #: 746

[10] John 19:30

[11] Mathew 24:3-31; Hebrews 12:2

[12] דבר: 1697 *Dabar* (daw-baw'); Noun Masculine, Strong #: 1697

[13] Hebrews 10:4-10; John 1:29

[14] John Calvin, *Institutes of the Christian Religion,* Printed at London by Arnold Hatfield, for Bonham Norton. 1599, *pp* 425-427

[15] Encyclopaedia Britannica Martin Luther German Religious Leader; Written By: Hans J. Hillerbrand Last Updated: November 6, 2019 See Article History

[16] Institutes of the Christian Religion Book II chapter 15, section 1,2

17. John 7: 15-18
18. John 21:25
19. Romans 5:16-21
20. Luke 6:6-10
21. John 3:31-35
22. Mathew 10:16-23; 13:39-57
23. Mathew 17:20; Mark 11:23
24. Mathew 21:19-21; Mark 11:13-21
25. Mathew 8:26-27; Mark 4:39; Luke 8:24-25
26. John 2:19-22
27. Mathew 24:15-25; Mark 13:14-23,
28. Mathew 24:3-14
29. 1 Samuel 19:19,20
30. 2 Kings 4:38
31. 2 Kings 2:3
32. 2 Kings 2:5
33. Acts 2:14-21
34. My paraphrase from the KJV and NIV Scripture quotations marked (NIV) are taken from the Holy Bible, New International Version®, NIV®. Copyright © 1973, 1978, 1984, 2011 by Biblica, Inc.™ Used by permission of Zondervan. All rights reserved worldwide. www.zondervan.com The "NIV" and "New International Version" are trademarks registered in the United States Patent and Trademark Office by Biblica, Inc.™
35. Genesis 21:14-20
36. 2 Corinthians 12:2-4
37. 2 Corinthians 11:14
38. Luke 4:41
39. 1 Samuel 3:4
40. 2 kings 20:1-5
41. Daniel 10: 2, 12
42. Mark 9:29

Notes

[43] 2 Kings 3:14–16
[44] 1 Samuel 10:5
[45] 1 Samuel 16:16,23
[46] Acts 16:25-34
[47] Benjamin B. Warfield, "Counterfeit Miracles", (CM). 1918
[48] Scripture taken from the Amplified Bible, Copyright © 1954, 1958, 1962, 1964, 1965, 1987 by The Lockman Foundation. Used by permission.
[49] Judges 13:20
[50] Acts 7:32
[51] Daniel 10:8
[52] Ezekiel 3:26
[53] Acts 10:10
[54] Mathew 16:5-12
[55] 1 Kings 18:17

www.ingramcontent.com/pod-product-compliance
Lightning Source LLC
Chambersburg PA
CBHW060325050426
42449CB00011B/2662